PROVENÇAL CUISINE

The cuisine of Provence and Nice comprises a separate galaxy in the variegated universe of French regional cooking. Its mainstays are garlic, olive oil and herbs, a triad that can be found in almost all savoury dishes of this superb gastronomic school. Inviting, easily digestible and appetising, it boasts a growing number of followers, captivated by its specialities, which are served with wines of exceptional character. We begin our tour with the sauces (from *aïoli* to *tapenade* to *rouille*), then moving on to delectable *hors d'oeuvres* (such as the delicious *berlingueto*), and continuing with hearty soups (among which we find *aïgo boulido, aïgo saou, bourride* and the renowned *bouillabaisse*). Next come the great fish dishes (such as *brandade, morue en raïto*) and main meat courses (*boeuf en daube, carbonnade, civet de lapin*), which are accompanied by tasty *tians*, vegetable and salad dishes (from *ratatouille* to the renowned *salade niçoise*), finishing up with dainty biscuits and cakes... The range is vast, allowing everyone, with little effort and ensured success – thanks to the series of photographs, illustrating stage by stage the procedures – to savour in the comfort of their own homes the delights of this great gastronomic tradition.

A DIETICIAN'S RATING

From the dietician's point of view, the cuisine of the French Midi represents a true Mediterranean approach to gastronomy which also incorporates dietetics.

This is due to their use of certain spices and to the great fishing tradition, but especially to the use of olive oil as the basis for providing fat content.

We here remind the reader what the mainstays of the Mediterranean diet are:
1) *a high presence of carbohydrates from cereals;*
2) *a fat content guaranteed by the consumption of olive oil as well as by the fats in fish and white meats;*
3) *a considerable intake of fibre from vegetables and fruit.*

It is clear that, even with such characteristics, we could "sell ourselves" to over-seasoned dishes, to an excessive use of hors d'oeuvres, side dishes and desserts which are undeniably overloaded.

In any case, we may conclude with the affirmation that here we have, by and large, a dietetic cuisine.

Aïoli

🍳⏱20'   6 ✸✸   Kcal 143 P 4 F 13   ⚖

| 6-7 cloves of garlic
3 egg yolks | Olive oil | |

1 Peel the garlic, eliminating the young shoot. Chop up finely.
Put in a bowl with a pinch of salt and the yolks at room temperature.
Beat briefly with a wooden spoon. Leave 5 minutes to rest.

2 Gradually whisk in a glass-and-a-half of olive oil, continuously beating in the same direction. Add a pinch of pepper (if liked) and whisk the sauce stiff.

This is very good with fish, meat and salads. You can blend it in a food processor.

Anchoïade

Rinse the anchovies under running cold water. Bone and fillet them.

Peel the garlic and chop finely (in the food processor, if you wish).

Add the anchovies, mashed with a fork, pour over a glass of olive oil and blend in thoroughly, adding a pinch of ground black pepper and one of salt (only if the anchovies are fresh).

Add a sprig of chopped parsley, stir and finish off the sauce with a few drops of vinegar (if liked).

Perfect for serving on pasta, spreading on bread croutons, together with white or red meats, and as a dressing for raw salad vegetables.

🍴⏱ 15'　　　　4 ✸✶

12-16 anchovies
   (preferably fresh, but salted ones
   are fine)
3-4 cloves of garlic
Parsley
Vinegar (optional)
Olive oil

Kcal 222 P 10 F 19

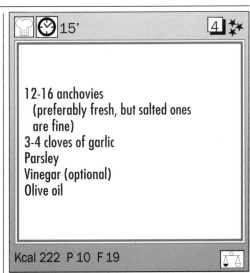

Tapenade

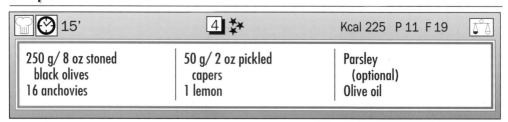

🍳 ⏲ 15'   4 ✹✹   Kcal 225   P 11   F 19   ⚖

250 g/ 8 oz stoned black olives 16 anchovies	50 g/ 2 oz pickled capers 1 lemon	Parsley (optional) Olive oil

1 Clean, bone and fillet the anchovies. Chop in a food processor, together with the black olives, cut to pieces, and the drained capers (called *tapeno* in Provence).

Place the mixture in a bowl and stir in 10-12 tablespoons of olive oil, the juice of a lemon and a pinch of pepper.

2 The *Tapenade*, as it is classically known, is ready. It should be a thick, smooth, dense paste. If you like, you may add aroma with a sprig of parsley or thyme and a bay leaf, finely chopped.

This is to be served with raw and boiled vegetables, but is also ideal on fish. It is particularly delicious with raw tuna fish (p. 39).

Provençal sauces, highly rated by Frédéric Mistral, truly seem to ooze sun, sea, grass and flowers. Besides those described in this book, we wish to draw your attention to melet, *similar to the* pissalat *in Nice. This consists in the pickled fry of various fish species (anchovies and sardines among them), bottled in brine with herbs and mashed to a paste. Then again, there is* saussoun, *characteristic of Roquebrune in the Var département, made up of shelled and blanched almonds, pound in a mortar with the fillets of 2-3 anchovies, a sprig of wild fennel and 4-5 mint leaves, and blended with some olive oil. It is quite delicious as a spread.*

Sauce toulonnaise is excellent: fry a finely chopped onion in olive oil until slightly coloured, add a glass of white wine, 4 ripe tomatoes (reduced to pulp), 2 cloves of garlic, a sprig each of parsley and basil, salt and pepper. The sauce is ready after it has simmered for half an hour.

Tasty is, of course, the sauce verte de Martigues, *based on herbs (chervil, parsley and tarragon) mixed with young spinach leaves, all pound in a mortar with a handful of capers, a few gherkins, 4 anchovy fillets and the yolks of 2 hard-boiled eggs and blended together with olive oil and a few drops of vinegar.*

This is delicious with boiled meats and fish.

Berlinguet eggs

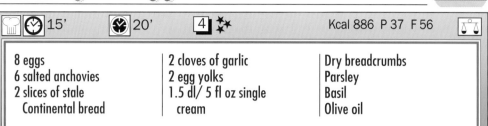

🍳⏱ 15'	❄ 20'	4 ✲✲	Kcal 886 P 37 F 56	⚖

8 eggs	2 cloves of garlic	Dry breadcrumbs
6 salted anchovies	2 egg yolks	Parsley
2 slices of stale	1.5 dl/ 5 fl oz single	Basil
Continental bread	cream	Olive oil

1 Soak the bread in the cream. Boil the eggs (7 minutes), shell and halve. Scoop out the yolks and place in a food processor.

3 Place in a bowl and amalgamate with a pinch of salt and pepper and the raw egg yolks.

2 Rinse, bone and fillet the anchovies. Add to the processor with a sprig each of parsley and basil, the peeled garlic and the bread, squeezed of excess cream (put this cream aside).
Beat gently until the mixture is smooth.

4 Stuff the boiled eggs with the mixture and arrange in a greased oven dish sprinkled with dry breadcrumbs and the re-served cream. Bake at 190-200 °C (375-400 °F / Gas Oven Mark 56) for 10 minutes.

Excellent as an hors d'oeuvre, it may be served on a buffet table.

Pissaladière

| 🍴⏱ 40'+1h | ✳ 30'+20' | 4 ✪✪ | Kcal 704 P 18 F 29 | ⚖ |

Pastry:	Topping:	1 clove of garlic
450 g/ 1 lb flour	4-5 ripe tomatoes	plus 1 to garnish
Baking powder	1 onion	(optional)
(1 sachet or 2 tsp.)	7-8 anchovies	Basil
Olive oil	Stoned black olives	Olive oil

Mix the flour with the baking powder, a pinch of salt, 4 tablespoons of olive oil and a glass of water, kneading until smooth. Leave to rest for an hour.

Rinse and fillet the anchovies. Peel the onion and chop finely. Peel and seed the tomatoes. Crush the garlic and sauté gently in 3-4 tablespoons of oil (remove as soon as it begins to colour).

Gently fry the onion, add the roughly chopped tomatoes and allow to reduce over gentle heat. After about 20 minutes, add the anchovy fillets and allow to disintegrate into the mixture. Roll out the pastry about half-an-inch thick and divide into four circles. Spread the prepared mixture over it, adding a handful of olives.

Bake at 220 °C (425 °F or Gas Oven Mark 7) for 20 minutes.

Serve garnished with basil and (if liked) a thinly sliced, raw clove of garlic.

Marinated sardines

Clean the sardines, discarding the entrails. Rinse and dry.
Peel the garlic and slice thinly.
Cut the lemon into wedges. Rinse the tomatoes, cut in half, seed and roughly chop.

Pour 5 tablespoons of olive oil into an oven dish or tin, together with a full glass of wine, a tablespoon of vinegar, a sprig of parsley, a little fennel, the bay leaves, a pinch of salt and a few black pepper corns.
Stir over a lively flame. Add the tomatoes, garlic and lemon.
At this stage, let it all simmer for about twenty minutes. In the meanwhile, brown the sardines in 6-7 tablespoons of oil, turning them over carefully.
Drain and sprinkle with salt.
Place in a serving dish, pour the marinade over and serve.

20' 25' 4

1 kg/ 2¼ lb sardines
3 ripe tomatoes
8 cloves of garlic
2 bay leaves
Dried wild fennel (and/or seeds)
Parsley
1 lemon
Dry white wine
Wine vinegar
Olive oil

Kcal 488 P 34 F 28

This dish is served cold as an hors d'oeuvre, preferably a few days after cooking.

Aïgo boulido

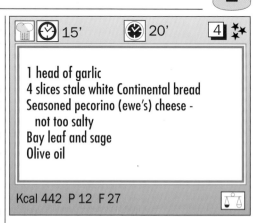

Place the peeled cloves of garlic in a pan with half a litre (one pint) of water and a pinch of salt.

Put on the lid and boil for 15 minutes. In the meanwhile, toast the bread slices and dredge with grated pecorino cheese.

Take the pan off the heat, remove the garlic and crush it with the prongs of a fork. Replace in the boiling water with a sprig of sage, a bay leaf, salt and pepper.

Line each soup bowl with the bread, pour on the *aïgo boulido* and drizzle over a spoon of raw, unheated olive oil.

This simple, aromatic, wholesome soup may be savoured just as it is, piping hot, or else placed in the oven for a moment and allowed to dry out slightly, especially on the surface.

🍳🕐 15'	✳ 20'	4 ✳✳

1 head of garlic
4 slices stale white Continental bread
Seasoned pecorino (ewe's) cheese - not too salty
Bay leaf and sage
Olive oil

Kcal 442 P 12 F 27

Aïgo saou

Trim and clean the vegetables. Split open the fish and remove the entrails. Scale, rinse and cut into pieces.

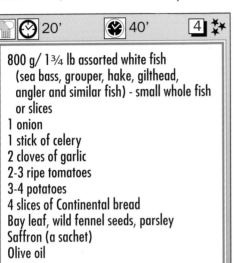

🍳 ⏰ 20'   ✺ 40'   4 ✹✹

800 g/ 1¾ lb assorted white fish
  (sea bass, grouper, hake, gilthead,
  angler and similar fish) - small whole fish
  or slices
1 onion
1 stick of celery
2 cloves of garlic
2-3 ripe tomatoes
3-4 potatoes
4 slices of Continental bread
Bay leaf, wild fennel seeds, parsley
Saffron (a sachet)
Olive oil

Kcal 584 P 40 F 12

Place the pieces in a pan with chunks of peeled potatoes, the sliced onion, the celery cut into short lengths, the diced tomatoes, the peeled garlic, a teaspoon of fennel seeds and a bay leaf.

Season with salt and pepper, pour over 2-3 tablespoons of olive oil and add 4 tablespoons of hot water in which you have dissolved the saffron powder. Put on the lid and boil vigorously for half-an-hour.

Pour the soup and vegetables over slices of toasted bread laid in the bottom of each soup bowl or in a tureen. The fish is to be served separately, well drained, and, just like the soup, sprinkled with chopped parsley.

Aïgo saou *(or "salted water" in Provençal) can also be made with seafood. Although originally it was served as a soup course, nowadays it may be served as a splendid luncheon dish.*

Aïgo saou d'iou

Another delicious, aromatic soup, literally called "eggs in salted water".

Rub the bread slices with a cut clove of garlic and toast in a heated oven. Clean the onion and leeks and chop finely. Fry gently with the peeled, finely sliced garlic in 5 tablespoons of oil until lightly coloured.
Add the washed tomatoes, seeded and roughly chopped, and the bouquet garni. Pour over 2 litres (2 quarts) of salted water, cover with the lid and simmer for half-an-hour. Add the peeled, sliced potatoes. Continue cooking for a further twenty minutes, after adding the saffron, salt and pepper.
Discard the bouquet garni, and take the pan off the heat. Place the toasted bread slices on the bottom of the soup bowls and break an egg into each.
The heat of the soup will immediately set them, just like with poached eggs. Pour over the soup.
Serve hot, offering grated Parmesan cheese separately for those who prefer it.

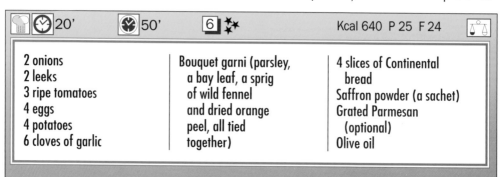

	20'		50'	6			Kcal 640 P 25 F 24	

2 onions 2 leeks 3 ripe tomatoes 4 eggs 4 potatoes 6 cloves of garlic	Bouquet garni (parsley, a bay leaf, a sprig of wild fennel and dried orange peel, all tied together)	4 slices of Continental bread Saffron powder (a sachet) Grated Parmesan (optional) Olive oil

Bourride ▶

Slit the fish open and remove the entrails. Scale and wash. Clean the cuttlefish, too, and cut it up with the assorted fish into pieces, but leave the white fish whole.
Peel and slice the onion and leek. Fry briefly, together with the garlic, a sprig of parsley, a teaspoon of fennel seeds and a bay leaf, in 3-4 tablespoons of oil. Add the cleaned, diced tomatoes. After 10 minutes, add the chunks of assorted fish and season with salt, pepper and hot red pepper. Stir once more, then, after 15 minutes, cover with hot water and a glass of wine.
After boiling for 10 minutes, draw the pan off the heat and purée the solid contents in a *mouli légumes* or rub through a sieve. Replace in the pan and bring to the boil once more. Add the pieces of cuttlefish and the saffron powder. Put on the lid and simmer, now and again topping up with hot water so as to keep the *bourride* quite fluid. After about 20 minutes, add the peeled potatoes.
In the meanwhile, toast the bread.
A quarter-of-an-hour before the dish finishes cooking, add the other fish. Finally, with the aid of a slotted spoon, remove the whole fish and the cuttlefish and arrange with the potatoes in a serving dish.
Place a slice of bread in each soup bowl, cover with *aïoli*, and pour over lots of the hot fish liquor.

Just like aïgo saou, bourride *started out as a soup course, but it is now eaten as a luncheon plate.*

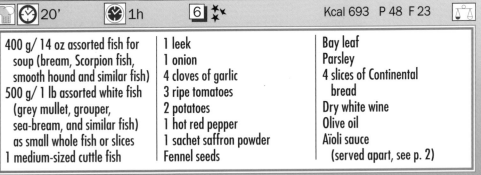

| 🍲 ⏰20' | ⏲1h | 6 ✨✨ | Kcal 693 P 48 F 23 | ⚖ |

400 g/ 14 oz assorted fish for soup (bream, Scorpion fish, smooth hound and similar fish)	1 leek	Bay leaf
	1 onion	Parsley
	4 cloves of garlic	4 slices of Continental bread
500 g/ 1 lb assorted white fish (grey mullet, grouper, sea-bream, and similar fish) as small whole fish or slices	3 ripe tomatoes	Dry white wine
	2 potatoes	Olive oil
	1 hot red pepper	Aïoli sauce (served apart, see p. 2)
	1 sachet saffron powder	
1 medium-sized cuttle fish	Fennel seeds	

Bouillabaisse

 30' 40' 6 * Kcal 597 P 45 F 27

800 g/ 1¾ lb assorted fish for soup (mullet, conger eel or razor-clams, Scorpion fish or gurnard, angler, scorpion fish, mackerel, weever, etc.) 4-5 red mullet (surmullet)	1 small lobster 1 striped bream or smooth hound, about 200 g/ 8 oz 1 leek 1 spring onion (scallion) 1-2 cloves of garlic	300 g/ 12 oz puréed tomato Chopped parsley 1 or 2 sachets of saffron powder 6 slices Continental bread Olive oil

Who, on holiday in the Midi, has not tried this, either as a rich stew or as a soup of fish and vegetables, flavoured with spices, in particular saffron? Nowadays it can even be bought pre-cooked and frozen.

1 The fish must be trimmed, washed and cut to pieces and the lobster split open lengthways.

3 Add all the fish, season with salt and pepper and dilute with 8 tablespoons of hot water. Stir well.

2 Finely chop up the leek and onion, fry gently until lightly coloured in 5 or 6 tablespoons of oil. Add the garlic and the puréed tomatoes and allow the flavours to blend over a gentle heat.

4 Add the saffron, parsley and a trickle of olive oil. Cook over medium heat for 30 minutes. Put the toasted bread slices into the soup tureen and cover with the *bouillabaisse*.

Pâtes à la rouille

Rouille *is a typical Provençal sauce, ideal for flavouring soups, fish, shellfish and also, such as in this case, as a refined dressing to serve on pasta. A boiled potato as a thickening for the sauce can, if you like, be added with fish dishes.*

⏱ 20'+10'   ❄ 12'   4 ✶✶

To make the rouille:

3 cloves of garlic
2 egg yolks
Saffron (a sachet)
Olive oil

To make the pasta:

350 g/ ¾ lb egg tagliatelle
500 g/ 1 lb mussels and baby clams
200 g/ 8 oz shrimp tails and young squid
3 cloves of garlic
Basil
1 dl/ 3 fl oz single cream
Olive oil

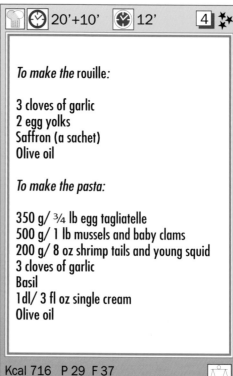

Kcal 716   P 29   F 37

1 To make the *rouille,* peel the garlic, chop it up very finely (you may use a food processor) and work it into the egg yolks with a pinch each of salt and pepper and the saffron powder. When the mixture is smooth and runny, leave to rest for 10 minutes.

2 Gradually drip in a glass of olive oil, stirring with a wooden spoon (or a whisk), always in the same direction.

Now let us turn to preparing the pasta dish. Clean the squid. Rinse the mussels and baby clams and place them in a pan with a little oil to cover the bottom.
Let them open up over low heat, then take them out of their shells and filter the liquor in the pan.
Return the molluscs to it with the shrimp tails, squid, 2 tablespoons of olive oil, the cream, 5 tablespoons of *rouille,* a few chopped basil leaves and the garlic. Reduce over a slow flame until you have an oily sauce.
Season with salt and pepper.
Meanwhile, cook the tagliatelle, draining the pasta while still firm to the bite.
Flavour briefly in the sauce in the pan (first remove the garlic) and serve immediately.

Lentil soup

Toast the bread. Wash the vegetables. Cut the tomatoes in half and seed them.

Peel the leek and onion, chop them up finely and colour slightly, together with the peeled garlic, in 3-4 tablespoons of oil. After 5 minutes, add the tomatoes and a bay leaf.

Stir and allow the flavours to blend for 5 minutes more.

Pour over 2 litres (2 quarts) hot water, add the lentils, sausage (if a "heartier" version is called for) and the peeled potatoes, cut into rounds or small chunks.

Bring slowly to the boil, cover with the lid and allow to simmer for about an hour.

When ready, take out the sausage (it can be served separately) and purée the soup

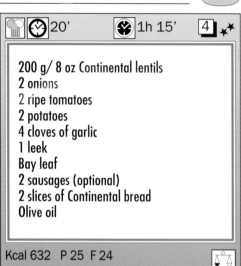

🕐 20'	✳ 1h 15'	4 ★★

200 g/ 8 oz Continental lentils
2 onions
2 ripe tomatoes
2 potatoes
4 cloves of garlic
1 leek
Bay leaf
2 sausages (optional)
2 slices of Continental bread
Olive oil

Kcal 632 P 25 F 24

in a *mouli légumes*, or rub through a sieve.

Place the soup in bowls with croutons of diced bread.

Pea soup

Peel the onion and leek. Chop finely, together with the garlic.

Allow to colour slightly in 3-4 tablespoons of oil, then add the rinsed (undried) peas

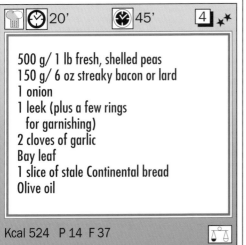

🎩 ⏰ 20'　　🕐 45'　　④ ✱✶

500 g/ 1 lb fresh, shelled peas
150 g/ 6 oz streaky bacon or lard
1 onion
1 leek (plus a few rings
　for garnishing)
2 cloves of garlic
Bay leaf
1 slice of stale Continental bread
Olive oil

Kcal 524　P 14　F 37

and the bay leaf. Briefly allow the flavours to blend. Pour over 2 litres (2 quarts) of cold water and add the diced bread and bacon.

After seasoning with salt and pepper, put on the lid and cook for a good half-hour. Then purée the soup solids in the *mouli légumes* (or rub through a sieve) and return to the stock, allowing it to thicken for a moment.

Pour the purée into the soup bowls. Garnish with rings of leek and sprinkle (if you like) with freshly ground pepper.

This soup can also be made out of season with dried peas (about 400 g/ 14 oz) instead of fresh ones. In that case, the cooking time must be lengthened to about an hour and hot water must be added during this time.

Soupe au pistou

Pistou is a sauce based on pound garlic and basil, blended with olive oil. It is used in Provence to soften and flavour soups and vegetables.

1 To make the *pistou*, wash, seed and peel the tomatoes (if you wish to include them). Rinse and dry the basil and remove the stems. Blend carefully in a food processor together with the peeled garlic, roughly chopped tomatoes and a pinch of salt and pepper.

2 Place the mixture in a bowl and gradually blend in the Parmesan and 12-15 tablespoons of olive oil, stirring all the time until the *pistou* thickens nicely. Leave a few minutes to rest.
Now prepare the soup. Rinse the tomatoes, top and tail the beans and peel the potatoes. Peel the onion and leek, slice finely and brown slowly in the melted butter.

Add the chopped-up tomatoes and potatoes and the green beans cut into short lengths.
Season with salt and pepper. Pour over half a litre (one pint) of vegetable stock and leave to cook over very gentle heat for about three quarters of an hour, adding more stock if necessary, a little at a time.
Serve the soup hot with the *pistou* separately so that each diner can help himself as he likes. A trickle of olive oil on top makes a nice finish.

In order to make the vegetable stock, boil a carrot, an onion, a rib of celery and a tomato in slightly salted water for a bare half an hour (or use a stock cube).

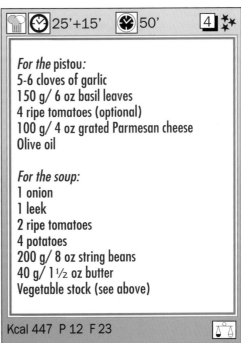

🕐 25'+15'   ❀ 50'   4 ✷✷

For the pistou:
5-6 cloves of garlic
150 g/ 6 oz basil leaves
4 ripe tomatoes (optional)
100 g/ 4 oz grated Parmesan cheese
Olive oil

For the soup:
1 onion
1 leek
2 ripe tomatoes
4 potatoes
200 g/ 8 oz string beans
40 g/ 1½ oz butter
Vegetable stock (see above)

Kcal 447 P 12 F 23

Haricot bean soup

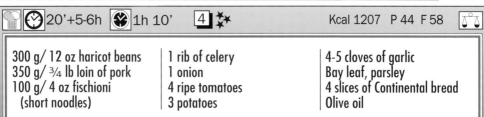

🕐 20'+5-6h ✻ 1h 10' 4 ✤✤ Kcal 1207 P 44 F 58

300 g/ 12 oz haricot beans	1 rib of celery	4-5 cloves of garlic
350 g/ ¾ lb loin of pork	1 onion	Bay leaf, parsley
100 g/ 4 oz fischioni	4 ripe tomatoes	4 slices of Continental bread
(short noodles)	3 potatoes	Olive oil

1 Soak the beans 5-6 hours. Rinse, peel and seed the tomatoes. Chop roughly. Peel the potatoes.
Peel the onion and chop finely. Repeat with the garlic and a sprig of parsley.

2 Put the pork in a saucepan with the celery in pieces and a bay leaf and cover with cold water.
Bring to the boil and simmer for half an hour, then add the drained beans and a pinch of salt. After a further 20 minutes, add the potatoes, whole.

3 Fry the chopped garlic, onion and parsley in 3-4 tablespoons of oil. Add the tomato and 8 tablespoons of the bean stock after 5 minutes.
Allow to reduce for 5-6 minutes, then pour in the contents of the saucepan (known as *lou fricholou* in Provençal), together with a pinch of pepper. Stir. Add the pasta and bring to the boil. Toast the bread.

4 Remove the piece of pork and cut it into strips before returning it to the pan.

Pour the soup into the soup bowls. Crumble the toast over and finish with a trickle of olive oil.

If a heartier version is preferred, substitute the loin of pork with a pig's trotter, to be boned once cooked.

Rabbit soup

1 Bone the rabbit, putting aside the head and bones. Cut the flesh into bite-sized pieces.

Cut the prosciutto into strips and brown in 3 tablespoons of oil, together with the crushed head and bones. After 15 minutes, pour on 2 litres (2 quarts) of hot water and bring to the boil.

While the stock is boiling, toast the unpeeled garlic and onion under the grill. As soon as they turn brown, add to the pan and put on the lid.

Leave an hour to simmer. Throw in a sprig of thyme.

2 In the meanwhile, peel and dice the carrot and celeriac.

Rinse, dry and slice the cauliflower.

Filter the rabbit stock, discarding any solids.

3 Brown the rabbit meat in 2 tablespoons of olive oil.

Pour in the stock and add the carrot and celeriac, the cauliflower, potato, courgette (zucchini), crushed cloves of garlic and a pinch of salt and pepper.

Cover with the lid and allow to simmer half an hour.

Now toast the bread.

4 Reduce both the potato and the courgette to pulp and then add the pasta to the pan and cook until it is *al dente*.

Lay the toast in the bottom of the soup bowls, sprinkle with Parmesan cheese and pour on the soup.

Scatter pieces of rabbit over the top and serve immediately.

  25'   2h 4 ✦✦ Kcal 774 P 49 F 35

The forequarters (or half) of a rabbit, 7-800 g/ 1½-1¾ lb 100 g/ 4 oz short pasta 2 slices prosciutto 1 carrot	1 onion A head of garlic, plus 4 cloves 1 potato 1 courgette (zucchini) 1 celeriac	1 wedge of cauliflower Thyme 4 slices of Continental bread Grated Parmesan Olive oil

Mussels "à la Provençale"

Peel the garlic, wash a large bunch of parsley, and chop together finely (use the food processor if you like) and blend in the softened butter and a pinch of salt. Scrape the mussels, tear off the "threads" and wash them under cold, running water. Put the mussels into a pan with a little olive oil and cook quickly over a high flame until they open. Discard any that remain closed. Put some of the garlic and parsley flavour butter onto the half shells containing the mussels. Arrange in an oven dish, put them in the oven and brown under the grill for 2 to 3 minutes.

As an alternative, blanch a generous kilogram (2¼ lb) of spinach leaves in a very little salted water. Drain after 5 minutes, chop finely and sauté with some chopped garlic and parsley, 3 tablespoons of olive oil, and a pinch each of salt, pepper and grated nutmeg. Stuff the molluscs with a third of the fried mixture and lay them on a layer of spinach in a greased oven dish. Cover with the remaining spinach, aromatised with wild fennel, a bay leaf and thyme. Bake briefly in the oven and serve.

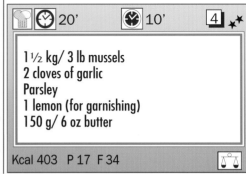

🕐 20'   ⊗ 10'   4 ✦

1½ kg/ 3 lb mussels
2 cloves of garlic
Parsley
1 lemon (for garnishing)
150 g/ 6 oz butter

Kcal 403   P 17   F 34

Octopus "en daube"

Trim the octopus and rinse in cold running water. Cut into pieces, including the tentacles.
Marinate with the bouquet garni and salt and pepper in 4 glasses of wine for 3 hours.
Drain, setting aside the solid marinated ingredients.
Peel an onion and chop finely with the carrot.
Fry until coloured in 4 tablespoons of oil in a pan, adding strips of lard. When the latter has browned, add the rinsed, seeded and roughly chopped tomatoes, well drained of their liquid.
Stir and add the filtered marinade, together with the garlic, the bouquet garni and the peeled half-onion, stuck with 3 cloves.
Cover the pan with the lid and cook over a very slow flame for one-and-a-half hours, until the octopus has become tender. Allow to cool in the cooking liquor.

25'+3h 1h 40' 4

About 1 kg/ 2 lb octopus (preferably small)
1 ½ onions
2 cloves of garlic
1 carrot
3 ripe tomatoes
100 g/ 4 oz lard or fatty bacon
1 bouquet garni (parsley, thyme, bay leaf, wild fennel)
3 cloves
Dry white wine
Olive oil

Kcal 543 P 26 F 37

Then reheat to lukewarm over a very low flame, removing the onion and garlic before serving.

Cuttlefish in their ink

Clean the cuttlefish and discard the bone, but keep the ink bladders. Wash and remove the fins and tentacles, setting them aside.

Lightly flour the cuttlefish "stalks" and brown in 3-4 tablespoons of oil over medium heat for about twenty minutes.

🍽️ ⏱️ 25' ❄️ 50' 4 ★★

4 cuttlefish,
    about 900 g/ 2 lb
1 onion
4 cloves of garlic
Bay leaf
Wild fennel (stamens
    or seeds)
Flour
Dry white wine
Olive oil
Vegetable stock (p. 21)

Kcal 371 P 29 F 18

In the meantime, peel an onion and chop in a food processor with the finely chopped garlic, the fins and the tentacles. Add the mixture to the pan containing the cuttlefish, together with a bay leaf and a teaspoon of fennel.

Season with salt and pepper. Allow the flavours to blend over gentle heat.

After a quarter-hour, pour over a glass of wine and reduce it over a low flame. Dilute the ink from the fish in the vegetable stock and gradually add to the pan over the flame, two tablespoons at a time.

Reduce until the sauce is nice and thick.

Serve, decorating the dish as you like.

Niçoise salt cod (Brandade)

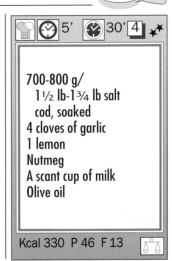

Blanch the salt cod for 5 minutes.
Trim, and eliminate the skin.
Heat 3-4 tablespoons of oil and add the fish.
Throw in the peeled garlic and, shaking the pan in a circular motion, allow the fish to absorb the flavour over gentle heat.
Continue shaking the pan while the fish cooks, never allowing it to reach boiling point.
After 3-4 minutes, add a drop of milk, still shaking the pan in a circular movement until it has been absorbed.
Continue in this way, alternating olive oil and milk until the latter is all used up. Flavour with a pinch of nutmeg.
Present the *brandade*, creamy and hot, with potatoes and mayonnaise, on a serving dish.

🍳 ⏱5' ❄30' 4 ✦✦

700-800 g/
  1½ lb-1¾ lb salt
  cod, soaked
4 cloves of garlic
1 lemon
Nutmeg
A scant cup of milk
Olive oil

Kcal 330 P 46 F 13

Eels in wine sauce

| 🍶⏰ 30' | ✸ 1h 15' | 4 ✴✴ | | Kcal 725 P 33 F 50 | ⚖ |

800 g/ 2 lb medium-sized eel	2 spring onions	Lemon rind
1 ripe tomato	(scallions)	Flour
1 leek	100 g/ 4 oz mushrooms	Sugar
1 onion	1 clove	Red wine
1 stick of celery	Bay leaf, thyme	Olive oil
4 cloves of garlic	Fennel seeds	Parsley

1 Wash the mushrooms and cut into pieces. Prepare the eels and cut into short lengths. Flour the pieces and brown them, together with the finely chopped onion and leek, in 4 tablespoons of oil. Season lightly with salt. Remove and drain the eels.

3 Brown the spring onions in 3-4 tablespoons of oil. Add the mushrooms and season with salt and pepper. Set aside and keep warm.

2 Pour 2-3 glasses of wine into the pan. Add a clove, a bay leaf, the celery in small rings, the roughly-chopped tomato, a pinch of sugar, salt and pepper, the lemon rind, the crushed garlic, the fennel seeds and a few thyme leaves.
Simmer 40 minutes.

4 Discard the bay leaf, fennel seeds and the rind. Replace the eels in the sauce in the pan and add the spring onions and the mushrooms. Allow the flavours to blend over low heat for a quarter-hour. Check for salt and pepper and serve the eels in their sauce. Sprinkle over some chopped parsley.

Salt cod "en raïto"

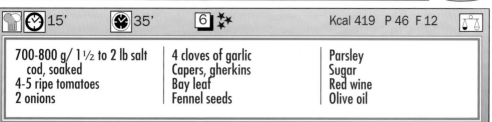

🎩 ⏱ 15'   ❂ 35'   6 ✿✿   Kcal 419 P 46 F 12   ⚖

700-800 g/ 1½ to 2 lb salt cod, soaked 4-5 ripe tomatoes 2 onions	4 cloves of garlic Capers, gherkins Bay leaf Fennel seeds	Parsley Sugar Red wine Olive oil

1 Scald the salt cod for 5 minutes. Trim the fish, eliminating the skin.
Wash the tomatoes, seed and chop coarsely. Peel the garlic and chop up finely with a sprig of parsley.

3 Pour over half a glass of wine, add a scant tablespoon capers and 12 gherkins, all chopped up, and reduce a quarter-hour over gentle heat.

2 Peel the onion, slice and brown in 3-4 tablespoons of oil in a pan. Add the tomato, the chopped garlic and parsley, a pinch each of salt and of pepper, a quarter teaspoon of sugar, a bay leaf and a pinch of fennel seeds.

4 Now dredge the cod in flour and brown in 4-5 tablespoons of olive oil in the frying pan.
After draining the fish, transfer to the sauce in the pan. Allow it to absorb the flavours of the prepared sauce over gentle heat for 5-6 minutes.

Mullet "à la Niçoise"

Rinse the anchovies, bone and fillet them. Clean the tomatoes, seed and chop roughly.
Squeeze the juice from one lemon.
Clean and scale the mullet, discarding the entrails. Season inside the body cavity with a pinch each of salt and pepper.
Coat lightly with flour. Brown over fierce heat in 5-6 tablespoons of oil, turning the fish over carefully because they are fragile. Place in a greased oven dish.
Arrange an anchovy fillet on each fish, surrounded by tomato.
Scatter some slices of lemon, olives, capers and parsley leaves on top. Sprinkle with lemon juice and bake in a pre-heated oven at 160 °C (300 °F or Gas Oven Mark 2) for 25 minutes.
Serve at once.

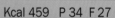

🍲 🕐 15' ⏣ 35' 4 ★★

8-10 medium-sized mullet
4-5 ripe tomatoes
3-4 lemons
4-5 anchovies
About 20 black olives
Capers, a handful
Parsley
Flour
Olive oil

Kcal 459 P 34 F 27

Foil-baked mullet parcels

Soak the breadcrumb in a little milk barely to cover. Clean and scale the mullet, discarding the entrails. Season inside the body cavity with a pinch each of salt and pepper and a drop of olive oil.

Squeeze the moisture from the breadcrumb and mix with the finely chopped garlic, the egg yolk, salt and pepper in a bowl. Use this mixture to stuff the fish.

Drizzle some olive oil over the fish. Wrap each one in a sheet of foil. Seal the "parcels" and bake in a cool oven (120 °C / 250 °F / Gas Oven Mark ½) for half-an-hour.

Open the "parcels" at the table and just savour them!

20' 30' 4

8-10 medium-sized mullet
1 clove of garlic
1 egg yolk
Chives
Milk
Breadcrumb (from two slices of bread)
Olive oil

Kcal 454 P 31 F 23

Stocaficada

| 🍞⏲15' | ⏱1h 10' | 4 ✦✦ | | Kcal 380 P 39 F 17 | ⚖ |

| 600-700 g/ about
1½ lb stockfish,
soaked
4-5 ripe tomatoes
1 potato | 1 onion
1 leek
2 cloves of garlic
12 black olives
Bouquet garni | (thyme, bay leaf,
parsley and fennel
or sweet
marjoram)
Olive oil |

1 Clean the stockfish and remove the skin.
Peel the onion and leek and slice. Brown in 3-4 tablespoons of olive oil.

3 Reduce over a low flame for about a quarter-hour. Add the fish. Season with a pinch of pepper, cover with the lid and simmer for a bare half-hour.

2 Throw in the bouquet garni, the sliced garlic and the cleaned, seeded and roughly chopped tomatoes.

4 Add the olives and the sliced potatoes. Cover with the lid once more and simmer for a further 20 minutes. Eliminate the bouquet garni and serve.

Salmon with dill

Sauté the salmon in 2-3 tablespoons of olive oil. Warm a glass of cream over gentle heat, but do not allow to boil.
Season with a pinch of salt, pepper and crumbled dill.
Lay the slices of salmon on the dinner plates and mask with the dill sauce. Serve with boiled courgettes (zucchini).

This dish is indeed delicate.

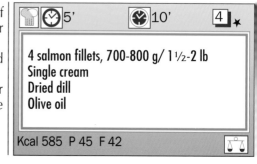

🍤 ⏱ 5'	❄ 10'	4 ★

4 salmon fillets, 700-800 g/ 1 ½-2 lb
Single cream
Dried dill
Olive oil

Kcal 585 P 45 F 42

Raw tuna

1 Trim the tuna fish and cut into strips. Dress with olive oil, salt and pepper. Sprinkle with the onion, dill and parsley, all chopped. Chill in the refrigerator for about 2 hours.

2 Sprinkle with lemon juice and mask in *tapenade* sauce (see page 4) before serving at table.
Present the dish arranged on a bed of lettuce leaves.

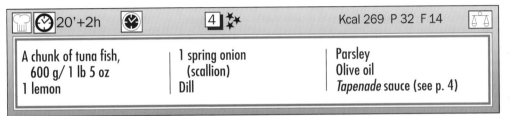

| 🕐 20'+2h | ✳ | 4 ✲✲ | Kcal 269 P 32 F 14 | ⚖ |

A chunk of tuna fish, 600 g/ 1 lb 5 oz	1 spring onion (scallion)	Parsley
1 lemon	Dill	Olive oil
		Tapenade sauce (see p. 4)

Tuna "à la Provençale"

🧑‍🍳⏱ 20'+1h	⏱ 1h	4 ✱✱		Kcal 455 P 49 F 19	⚖

A chunk of tuna fish, 800 g/ 2 lb 4-5 ripe tomatoes 1 onion	2 cloves of garlic Bouquet garni (bay leaf, wild fennel, parsley, thyme)	4 anchovies 1 lemon Dry white wine Olive oil

1 Rinse and fillet the anchovies. Wrap pieces of anchovy around the tuna and marinate for an hour in the lemon juice, the bouquet garni and 5-6 tablespoons of olive oil.
Every now and again, turn over the fish.

3 Throw in the tomatoes and crushed garlic and reduce over gentle heat.

2 Drain the tuna, setting aside the oil. Wash the tomatoes and chop roughly. Peel and chop the onion finely. Brown in the marinade oil.

4 After about 15 minutes, add to the tuna sauce.
Adjust for salt and pepper.
Now pour over a glass of white wine, put on the lid and leave to cook for another forty minutes over gentle heat.
Serve this flavoursome tuna fish covered in its delicious sauce.

Sardine "tian" with spinach

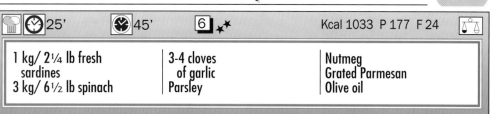

🍳⏱ 25'	✹ 45'	6 ⋆⋆	Kcal 1033 P 177 F 24	⚖

1 kg/ 2¼ lb fresh
  sardines
3 kg/ 6½ lb spinach
	3-4 cloves
	  of garlic
	Parsley
		Nutmeg
		Grated Parmesan
		Olive oil

1 Clean the sardines, discarding the entrails and bones. Dry them and open out flat.
Wash the spinach and plunge into boiling water with a pinch of salt for 7-8 minutes. Drain, but do not dry. Chop finely.

3 Lightly grease an oven dish and lay a bed of spinach in the bottom.
Place the sardines on a chopping board and put a teaspoon of sautéed spinach on each.
Fold over and arrange the sardines on the bed of spinach.

2 Flavour the spinach in 4-5 tablespoons of olive oil, seasoning with a pinch each of nutmeg, salt and pepper. After 10 minutes, add the garlic and a sprig of parsley, all finely chopped. Allow the spinach to absorb the flavour. Draw off the heat.

4 Cover with the remaining spinach and level off the surface.
Sprinkle with grated Parmesan cheese add a swirl of olive oil. Bake for about 20 minutes at 180 °C (350 °F or Gas Oven Mark 4).

Languedoc snails

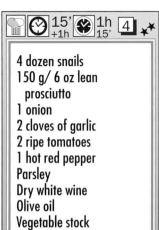

If you have gathered the snails yourself, follow the instructions given below for draining off the slime and scum.

If, on the other hand, you have, in all likelihood, bought them in a jar, soak them in cold water for at least an hour beforehand and follow the instructions printed on the packet.

Cut the ham into strips. Peel the garlic and onion, chop finely and brown in 3 tablespoons of oil.

Add the prosciutto, hot red pepper and tomatoes, seeded and roughly chopped.

Allow the flavours to blend,

then add the drained snails, 8 tablespoons of stock and a glass of wine.

Put on the lid and leave to

15' +1h 1h 15' 4

4 dozen snails
150 g/ 6 oz lean
    prosciutto
1 onion
2 cloves of garlic
2 ripe tomatoes
1 hot red pepper
Parsley
Dry white wine
Olive oil
Vegetable stock
    (see p. 21)

Kcal 447 P 25 F 30

simmer as slowly as possible for an hour, seasoning with salt and pepper.

Serve the snails in their shells, together with their sauce and a sprinkling of chopped parsley.

Put the snails under an upturned bucket with some bran and salad for 3-4 days.

Then wash them and place in cold water in a saucepan.

Cover with the lid, bring to the boil and simmer for half-an-hour. Skim the surface regularly.

Finally, take them out of their shells, wash them and rinse in vinegar.

Provençal snails

Regarding the cleaning and preparation of these molluscs, please see the previous recipe if you have gathered the snails yourself.

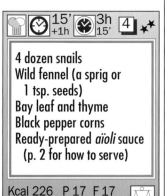

| | 15'
+1h | | 3h
15' | 4 | ** |

4 dozen snails
Wild fennel (a sprig or
1 tsp. seeds)
Bay leaf and thyme
Black pepper corns
Ready-prepared *aïoli* **sauce**
(p. 2 for how to serve)

Kcal 226 P 17 F 17

If, on the other hand, you have bought them in a jar, soak them in cold water an hour beforehand, as previously explained.
Follow the instructions printed on the packet.

Put the snails, cleaned out and drained, in 2 litres (2 quarts) of water in a pan. Bring slowly to the boil.

After a quarter-hour, add a pinch of salt, the fennel, the leaves from a twig of thyme, a bay leaf and also a teaspoon of black pepper corns.
Cover with the lid and cook very slowly for about 3 hours. Allow the snails to cool a little in their liquor, then serve them in their shells, offering *aïoli* sauce (see page 2) separately.

Boeuf en daube ▶

1 Peel the onions, sticking 3 or 4 cloves into one. Cut into wedges.
Clean the carrot and slice into rounds. Tie up the bouquet garni after washing and trimming the herbs.

2 Brown strips of the bacon in 4 table-spoons of oil with the onions, the carrot, the puréed tomato, the garlic, the bouquet garni, a little grated orange peel, a pinch of salt and a few peppercorns.
After 5-6 minutes, add the cubed steak and cover with red wine.
Put on the lid and bring quickly to the boil. Lower the flame and cook very slowly, for at least two and a half hours, keeping the lid on.
If necessary, more wine can be added. Adjust for salt and pepper.

Provençal cutlets

Lightly beat out the cutlets, rub them with garlic on both sides and sauté in 4 tablespoons of oil.
When they have coloured nicely, add the peeled onion, chopped up finely with a sprig of parsley and the needles from a twig of rosemary.
Pour over a glass of wine, seasoning with salt and pepper.
Cook about fifteen minutes, then pour on 8 tablespoons of stock and reduce completely. Draw the pan off the heat and add a beaten egg yolk, carefully binding the sauce.
Beat the other egg yolk, roll the cutlets in it, then lightly bread them on both sides.
Place them on a baking tray and put under the grill for three minutes each side. Serve with a green salad.

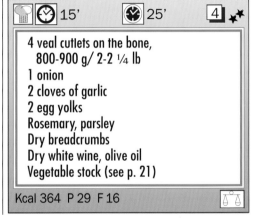

🍳🕐 15'	❀ 25'	4 ✴
4 veal cutlets on the bone, 800-900 g/ 2-2 ¼ lb		
1 onion		
2 cloves of garlic		
2 egg yolks		
Rosemary, parsley		
Dry breadcrumbs		
Dry white wine, olive oil		
Vegetable stock (see p. 21)		
Kcal 364 P 29 F 16		⚖

15'   2h 40'   4 ⋆⋆   Kcal 491 P 43 F 25

800 g/ 2 lb stewing steak	1 carrot	Orange peel
80 g/ 3 oz streaky bacon or lard	4 cloves of garlic	Cloves
200 g/ 8 oz puréed tomato	Bouquet garni (thyme, bay leaf, rosemary, parsley, sage)	Peppercorns Red wine
2 onions		Olive oil

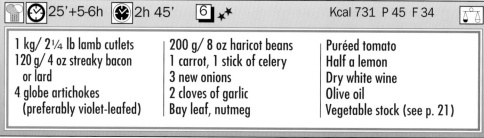

🍲 ⏰ 25'+5-6h	⏱ 2h 45'	6 ★★		Kcal 731 P 45 F 34	⚖

1 kg/ 2¼ lb lamb cutlets	200 g/ 8 oz haricot beans	Puréed tomato
120 g/ 4 oz streaky bacon	1 carrot, 1 stick of celery	Half a lemon
or lard	3 new onions	Dry white wine
4 globe artichokes	2 cloves of garlic	Olive oil
(preferably violet-leafed)	Bay leaf, nutmeg	Vegetable stock (see p. 21)

Carbonnade

1 Soak the beans for 5-6 hours. Lightly beat out the cutlets and rub both sides with garlic.
Lay them in a bowl, dress with a pinch of salt and pepper and a trickle of olive oil and set aside as the beans are soaking.

3 Cut the bacon into strips and brown in 4 or 5 tablespoons of oil
Add the lamb, a bay leaf, a pinch of grated nutmeg, the chopped carrot and celery, onion rings and 4 tablespoons of puréed tomato. Season with salt and pepper.

2 Boil the beans in plenty of lightly salted water in a covered saucepan over a very slow flame for about a half-hour.
Wash the artichokes, discard the stalks and slice them across the top.
Plunge into boiling, lightly salted water, soured with lemon juice, for 5-6 minutes.

4 Pour in 2 glasses of wine, put on the lid and leave to simmer for about 2 hours. Then add the beans and artichokes. Pour over 4 tablespoons of vegetable stock, adjust the salt and pepper and leave to cook slowly for a further 30 minutes.

This is quite a hearty dish, the more so if (as tradition has it) shoulder or leg of mutton is used instead of lamb.

Rabbit stew

🍳 ⏱ 25'+2h   ❄ 50'   ⟨4⟩ ✱✱   Kcal 433 P 45 F 18   ⚖

| 1 rabbit, 1.3 kg/ 2¾ lb
1 onion
2 scallions
Bay leaf, wild fennel, | sage and thyme,
plus a bouquet garni
of the same herbs
Flour | Red wine
Olive oil
Vegetable stock
(see p. 21) |

1 Wash the rabbit and divide into 10-12 pieces.
Marinate for 2 hours in ½ l (1 pt) wine, with the herbs, the new onions in rings and a pinch each of salt and pepper.

3 In a food processor, chop up the solid parts of the marinade, together with a glass of the reserved liquid marinade. Add to the rabbit. Reduce slowly and stir in 2 tablespoons of flour.

2 Peel the onion and colour lightly in 4-5 tablespoons of oil.
Add the drained pieces of rabbit, keeping the marinade aside.
Brown the rabbit.
Season with salt and pepper.

4 Add the bouquet garni and 8 tablespoons of stock. Simmer for half-an-hour. Add more hot stock, if necessary, adjusting for salt and pepper.

By tradition, the rabbit should cook in its own blood, but we opt for a lighter version.

Provençal rabbit

Wash and dry the rabbit. Divide into 10-12 pieces.
Brown in 4 tablespoons of oil, seasoning lightly with salt.

Pour off the oil and add a glass of stock, heating it over a moderate flame.
Roll the pieces of rabbit lightly in flour and return to the pan.
Allow the flavours to be absorbed, then pour over a glass of wine, adjusting for salt and pepper.
Add the cleaned, seeded, roughly chopped tomatoes, the garlic, black peppercorns and a teaspoon of mustard.
Cook the rabbit very slowly, adding more stock as necessary.
The rabbit should cook in about 50 minutes, all in all.
Filter the sauce and pour over the pieces of rabbit on the serving dish.
Serve with boiled green beans and salad.

25' +2h 50' 4 ★★

1 rabbit, 1.3 kg/ 2 ¾ lb
3 ripe tomatoes
2 cloves of garlic
Prepared mustard
Flour
Dry white wine
Olive oil
Vegetable stock
(see p. 21)

Kcal 468 P 46 F 18

Stuffed Guinea fowl

Soak the bread and the mushrooms separately in a little warm water for half an hour.

Prepare the bird for roasting - pluck and draw it, cut off the head and claws, and singe. Wash, dry and season it inside with salt and pepper.

Brown the garlic lightly in 3-4 tablespoons of oil, remove, and then, in the same oil, sauté the pork, breadcrumb and mushrooms after the liquid has been squeezed out.

Season with salt, pepper, a bay leaf (do not forget to then remove it) and some sprigs of thyme.

Douse with half a glass of Madeira and reduce for 15 minutes over gentle heat, checking for salt and pepper. Stuff the guinea fowl with the crumb mixture and tie it up with string.

Grease and season the bird on the outside with salt.

Place in a greased oven dish and roast for 40 minutes at 180 °C (350 °F or Gas Oven Mark 4).

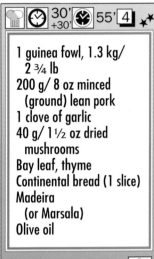

30'
+30' 55' 4

1 guinea fowl, 1.3 kg/ 2 ¾ lb
200 g/ 8 oz minced (ground) lean pork
1 clove of garlic
40 g/ 1 ½ oz dried mushrooms
Bay leaf, thyme
Continental bread (1 slice)
Madeira (or Marsala)
Olive oil

Kcal 588 P 59 F 22

Provençal omelette

Wash the tomatoes, seed and chop roughly. Peel and slice the onion. Allow to colour in 4-5 tablespoons of oil.

Add the tomatoes and the peeled and crushed garlic. Season freely with salt and pepper.
Cook very gently for about 15 minutes.
Add the beaten egg and a sprig of parsley with a couple of basil leaves, chopped up together.
Allow the omelette to set, turn over with the aid of a plate and leave to cook slowly, seasoning with salt and pepper.
Serve garnished with slices of ripe tomato and onion rings.

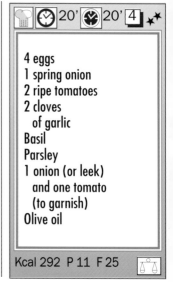

20' 20' 4

4 eggs
1 spring onion
2 ripe tomatoes
2 cloves
   of garlic
Basil
Parsley
1 onion (or leek)
   and one tomato
   (to garnish)
Olive oil

Kcal 292 P 11 F 25

Spiced omelette

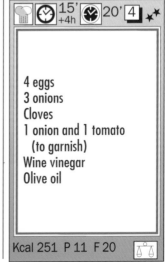

P eel the onions and stick each one with 2 or 3 cloves.
Leave for 4 hours in a bowl full of water in which you have dissolved a glass of vinegar.
Then blanch for 2-3 minutes in the same water. Drain.
Slice and allow to colour slightly in 3-4 tablespoons of oil.
Pour in the egg, beaten with a pinch of salt and pepper.
Cook the omelette, turning

it half way through with the aid of a plate.

This is eaten cold, garnished with slices of ripe tomato and onion rings.

15' +4h 20' 4 ★★

4 eggs
3 onions
Cloves
1 onion and 1 tomato (to garnish)
Wine vinegar
Olive oil

Kcal 251 P 11 F 20

Artichokes "à la barigoule"

Clean the artichokes, removing the stalks and tips of the prickly leaves. Turn them upside down and press down gently on a work surface to open them out a little.

Chop the garlic finely with a sprig of parsley, and mix in with the crumbed bread.

Peel the carrot and onion, chop finely and spread over the bottom of an oven dish with 4 tablespoons of oil.

Arrange the artichokes upright, sprinkle the crumb mixture over, and season each with a trickle of oil, salt and pepper. Pour over a glass of wine and cover the dish.

Bake in the oven at 140 °C (275 °F or Gas Oven Mark 1) for an hour-and-a-half.

🕛 25'   ❂ 1h 30'   4 ★★

8 violet-leafed globe artichokes
1 onion
1 carrot
2 cloves of garlic
Parsley
2 slices of stale
   Continental bread
Dry white wine
Olive oil

Kcal 369 P 11 F 10

Provençal vegetables "au gratin"

Wash the tomatoes, cut in half, seed and dice. Clean and trim the courgettes and cut into rounds. Peel the aubergines, slice and arrange on a plate. Sprinkle the slices with coarse salt and leave for a while under a weight until the bitter juices run out. Peel the onions and chop finely.

Place a layer in a greased oven dish, topped with a layer of tomatoes, one of courgettes and another of the aubergines, rinsed, drained, dried and diced.
Dress with a trickle of oil, and salt and pepper as you wish. Continue with layers in the same order until all the ingredients have been used up.

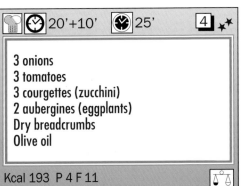

🍳 🕐 20'+10' 🕐 25' 4 ★★

3 onions
3 tomatoes
3 courgettes (zucchini)
2 aubergines (eggplants)
Dry breadcrumbs
Olive oil

Kcal 193 P 4 F 11

Dredge the surface with dry breadcrumbs, sprinkle over a little oil and bake for 25 minutes in the oven at 180 °C (350 °F or Gas Oven Mark 4).

Ratatouille Niçoise

Peel and slice the aubergine and arrange on a plate. Sprinkle the slices with coarse salt and leave for a while under a weight until the bitter juices run out.

🍳⏲ 25'+10'	❄ 30'	4 ✸✸

2 onions
2 sweet peppers
2 courgettes (zucchini)
5 ripe tomatoes
4-5 cloves of garlic
1 aubergine (eggplant)
Bouquet garni (bay leaf, basil, parsley, wild fennel, thyme)
Olive oil

Kcal 156 P 3 F 10

Peel and slice the onions. Wash the tomatoes, cut in half, seed and dice.
Clean and trim the courgettes. Dice, but do not peel.
Clean the peppers, remove the pith and seeds and cut into strips.
Rinse, drain, dry and dice the aubergines and put with the other vegetables in a pan with the bouquet garni, the garlic and 2 tablespoons of oil.
Leave half an hour to simmer, seasoning with salt and pepper.

The classic ratatouille, a traditional mixture of vegetables, is good either hot or cold. Serve it on its own (perhaps with couscous or bulghur wheat), or as a side dish to accompany meat or fish.

Mixed salad

Boil the eggs for 7 minutes, shell, allow to cool and cut into wedges.
Clean, wash and dry the salad leaves.
Rub the slices of bread (you can toast them, if you prefer) with a clove of garlic and dice.
Slice the remaining garlic very finely and place in a bowl with the salad and stoned olives.
Dress with oil, vinegar, salt and pepper.
Add the croutons and turn well.
Garnish with the wedges of hard-boiled egg and serve.

This salad is more nutritious with the boiled eggs (as in this case), but also with strips of lard or bacon, or else with seafood and shellfish. In this way, it becomes an excellent, very fresh luncheon dish.

🍳⏲ 20'	❄ 7'	4 ✦✸

500 g/ 1 lb mixed salad (a mix of rocket, dandelion, chicory, as you like)
2-3 slices of stale Continental bread
2-3 cloves of garlic
Black olives (2 dozen)
2 hard-boiled eggs (to garnish)
Red wine vinegar
Olive oil

Kcal 332 P 10 F 20

Salade Niçoise

Slit the anchovies open, discard the entrails and bones, rinse and fillet them.

Wash the artichokes, eliminate the stalks and spiky leaf ends.

Scald in lightly salted, boiling water, soured with lemon juice. Drain.

Boil the eggs (7 minutes), shell and cut into wedges.

Wash the sweet pepper and the tomatoes, cut in half and remove the seeds. Cut the former into strips and the latter into wedges.

Clean and rinse the lettuce. Do the same with the scallions, and cut them into thin rounds.

Last thing, wash the celery and cut into rounds.

In a salad bowl, place the lettuce leaves, tomatoes, sliced artichokes, the sweet pepper, a little drained and crumbled tuna fish, the celery and scallions.

Form another layer, finishing up with the eggs and olives on top.

Blend a tablespoon of vinegar in 6 tablespoons of oil and season with a pinch of salt and pepper.

Use to dress this most classical of salads and serve fresh and fragrant.

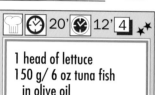

20' 12' 4

1 head of lettuce
150 g/ 6 oz tuna fish
  in olive oil
4 ripe tomatoes
1 sweet pepper
1 stick of celery
  with leaves
2 artichokes
2 scallions
4 eggs
4 anchovies
50 g/ 2 oz black olives
1 lemon
Vinegar
Olive oil

Kcal 492 P 33 F 32

Biscottins

Gradually grind the almonds finely in an electric grinder.
Pile 230 g (½ lb) of flour up on a pastry board, break the eggs into the well at the top and mix with your hands.
Work in the ground almonds and very finely grated lemon rind, with a

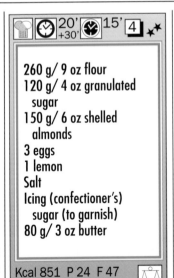

| 🍳 | ⏱ 20'
+30' | ❄ 15' | 4 | ★★ |

260 g/ 9 oz flour
120 g/ 4 oz granulated sugar
150 g/ 6 oz shelled almonds
3 eggs
1 lemon
Salt
Icing (confectioner's) sugar (to garnish)
80 g/ 3 oz butter

Kcal 851 P 24 F 47 ⚖

pinch of salt. Shape the dough into a ball and leave to rest for half-an-hour.

Roll out the pastry into a sheet about half-an-inch thick and cut out little rectangles of 2½ by ½ inch. Arrange them well apart on a buttered and floured baking tray and bake in a preheated oven at 180 °C (350 °F or Gas Oven Mark 4) for 15 minutes.
Serve them dusted with icing (confectioner's) sugar. They are excellent munched at teatime or with a glass of raisin wine.

Frangipane

Knead the flour with a pinch of salt and a teacup of water, and incorporate 125 g (4 oz) of the butter.

Shape into a ball and allow to rest for 30 minutes.

Roll out the pastry, place the rest of the butter in a block in the centre, fold over the edges and wrap the pastry around it. Roll out again.

Fold the bottom over and then one side over and roll it out again.

Repeat this operation 4 times. Allow to rest half-an-hour, then repeat the rolling out and folding over another 5 times.

Slowly whisk the sugar and flour with 2 beaten eggs in a pan.

Add the warm milk, still whisking, and bring to the boil. After 3 minutes, draw off the heat, turn into a bowl and allow to cool. Stir in the ground almonds.

Divide the pastry into two thin discs of equal size, about a quarter-inch thick and 10-12 inches in diameter.

Line the base of a pie plate with grease-proof paper and lay one disc on top. Spoon the custard into the centre, levelling it off and leaving a margin of over an inch all around.

Moisten this border and cover the plate with the other disc of pastry, sealing the edges with care. Cut off any pastry overlapping the edges.

Decorate the surface with the point of a knife and brush with beaten egg.

Leave a quarter-hour to rest, then bake for an hour in a pre-heated oven at 250 °C (475 °F or Gas Oven Mark 9).

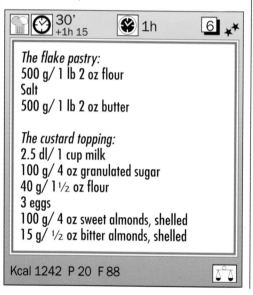

⏱ 30' +1h 15   ❁ 1h   6 ⭐⭐

The flake pastry:
500 g/ 1 lb 2 oz flour
Salt
500 g/ 1 lb 2 oz butter

The custard topping:
2.5 dl/ 1 cup milk
100 g/ 4 oz granulated sugar
40 g/ 1½ oz flour
3 eggs
100 g/ 4 oz sweet almonds, shelled
15 g/ ½ oz bitter almonds, shelled

Kcal 1242 P 20 F 88

Orange flower tart ▶

Preheat the oven to 100 °C (210 °F or Gas Oven Mark ½), then turn it off.

Heat the milk and dissolve the baking powder in it.

Just before it reaches the boiling point, add 100 g (4 oz) of granulated sugar, 220 g (½ lb) of flour, ¾ of the butter, the eggs, a pinch of salt and 5 or 6 drops of orange water. Stir carefully.

Draw off the heat as soon as it starts to thicken and stir with a wooden spoon until it becomes dense and springy.

Shape into a ball and put in the tepid oven for an hour.

The dough will double. Take it out, knead briefly and place in a buttered ring mould that has been floured and sprinkled with brown sugar.

Bake the cake for 20 minutes at 200 °C (400 °F or Gas Oven Mark 6).

Take out and remove the cake from the mould while hot.

Allow to cool a little before decorating the centre with whipped cream.

| 🧁⏱ 20'+1h | ❋ 20' | 4 ★★ | Kcal 1104 P 17 F 68 |

250 g/ 9 oz flour
A sachet of baking
   powder (16 g/ 2 tsp.)
2 eggs

3 dl/ 8 fl. oz. milk
100 g/ 4 oz brown sugar
120 g/ 4½ oz granulated
   sugar

Orange water
Salt
Whipped cream (to decorate)
120 g/ 4½ oz butter

Index

PROVENÇAL CUISINE

Project: Casa Editrice Bonechi
Series editor: Giovanna Magi
Publication manager: Alberto Andreini
Coordinator: Paolo Piazzesi
Layout and cover: Maria Rosanna Malagrinò
Make-up: Alberto Douglas Scotti
Editing: Costanza Marsili Libelli
Translation: Stephanie Johnson

Every recipe in this book has been tested by our cooks.
In the kitchen: Lisa Mugnai
Dietician: Dr. John Luke Hili

Photographs from the Archives of Casa Editrice Bonechi *taken by* Andrea Fantauzzo.

© by CASA EDITRICE BONECHI, Florence - Italy
E-mail: bonechi@bonechi.it   Internet: www.bonechi.it

Printed in Italy by Centro Stampa Editoriale Bonechi.

***